THE IMITATION OF JESUS

———————

A. Blake White

Other books by A. Blake White

The Newness of the New Covenant
The Law of Christ: A Theological Proposal
Galatians: A Theological Interpretation
*Abide in Him: A Theological Interpretation
of John's First Letter*
Union with Christ: Last Adam & Seed of Abraham
What is New Covenant Theology? An Introduction
Theological Foundations for New Covenant Ethics
The Abrahamic Promises in the Book of Galatians
Missional Ecclesiology

THE IMITATION OF JESUS

A. Blake White

5317 Wye Creek Drive, Frederick, MD 21703-6938
301-473-8781 | info@newcovenantmedia.com
www.NewCovenantMedia.com

The Imitation of Jesus

Copyright 2014 © A. Blake White

Published by: New Covenant Media
5317 Wye Creek Drive
Frederick, MD 21703-6938

Cover design by Matt Tolbert.

All rights reserved. No part of this publication may be produced, stored in a retrieval system, or transmitted in any form by any means, electronic, mechanical, photocopy, recording, or otherwise without the prior permission of the publisher, except as provided by USA copyright law.

Printed in the United States of America

ISBN 13: 978-1-928965-60-2

Unless otherwise noted, all Scripture quotations are taken from the Holman Christian Standard Bible®, Copyright © 1999, 2000, 2002, 2003, 2009 by Holman Bible Publishers. Used by permission. Holman Christian Standard Bible®, Holman CSB®, and HCSB® are federally registered trademarks of Holman Bible Publishers.

To Karis Ann,

I pray daily that God would grant you faith (Philip. 1:29) and give you the grace to make you consumed with making much of King Jesus in every way (Philip. 1:20-21).

Table of Contents

Table of Contents i
Introduction 1
The Imitation of Jesus 3
Objective Foundation 5
Love 11
New Testament Texts 13
I Have Left You an Example—John 13 15
Servants of All—Mark 10:42-45 19
The Jesus Mindset—Philippians 2:1-8 23
The "Pattern" of the Messiah—Galatians 6:2 27
Because Even Jesus—Romans 15:1-7 35
Imitate Me—1 Corinthians 9-11 41
Though He Was Rich— 2 Corinthians 8:9 47
As Christ Loved the Church—
Ephesians 4:32-5:1 and 5:25-26 49
He Left Us an Example—1 Peter 2:21-23 51
Conclusion 53
Scripture Index 57
Bibliography 61

Introduction

In his recent book, *Continuity and Discontinuity*, John Reisinger writes, "I fear that some New Covenant Theology people are neglecting the role of Christ as a sufficient moral example. They seem to want to create a *new* Old Covenant that is just as rule, or law, centered as the *old* Old Covenant."[1] I agree, and that is the reason for this booklet. I love this theme because I believe God loves this theme. It is all over the New Testament. This little book is a fresh exposition of nine passages of the New Testament. I dealt with one of the passages in *What is New Covenant Theology?*[2] and four of them in Part II of *Theological Foundations for New Covenant Ethics* on cruciform love,[3] which is a tad more accessible than the present work. It is my hope that this shorter work will be appealing to a broader audience. I also hope preachers and teachers will consider using these texts as the basis for a series or study on the imitation of Jesus, which is another way of teaching about biblical love.

---

[1] John G. Reisinger, *Continuity and Discontinuity* (Frederick, MD: New Covenant Media, 2011), 11.

[2] A. Blake White, *What is New Covenant Theology?: An Introduction* (Frederick, MD: New Covenant Media, 2013), 29-38.

[3] Ibid., *Theological Foundations for New Covenant Ethics* (Frederick, MD: New Covenant Media, 2013), 69-135.

The Imitation of Jesus

Evangelical theology tends to be reactionary. Often the motive for reactionary theology is pure since there is a lot of sub-biblical theology worthy of reaction. The downside is sometimes the theological pendulum swings too far and important biblical themes are ignored or neglected. The imitation of the self-giving love of Jesus is one such neglected theme. Jason Hood, in an important article called "The Cross in the New Testament," writes, "The biblical teaching on the imitation of the crucified Christ is the most neglected aspect of recent work on the NT message of the cross. This neglect is particularly acute among works produced in Reformed and evangelical circles."[4] He goes on to assert that "the imitation of Jesus, above all in the cross, consistently arises as one of the New Testament's primary applications of the meaning of the cross. Such cross-shaped missional suffering in the pattern of Jesus must be regarded as a crucial component for teaching the NT's message of the cross."[5]

This booklet will seek to exegetically vindicate Hood's comment by demonstrating that new covenant believers should seek to imitate Jesus' death in a host of diverse situations, ranging from "marriage to generosity, from

---

[4] Jason B. Hood, "The Cross in the New Testament: Two Theses in Conversation with Recent Literature (2000-2007)," *Westminster Theological Journal* 71 (2009): 286.

[5] Ibid., 287.

forgiveness to evangelism and pastoral care."[6] It will focus on nine key passages where the writers of the New Testament appeal to the example of Jesus' self-giving love as the norm for Christians.

---

[6] Jason B. Hood, *Imitating God in Christ: Recapturing a Biblical Pattern* (Downers Grove, IL: IVP Academic, 2013), 135, 136, 214; also Richard A. Burridge, *Imitating Jesus: An Inclusive Approach to New Testament Ethics* (Grand Rapids: Eerdmans, 2007), 146, 148; Michael J. Gorman, *Cruciformity: Paul's Narrative Spirituality of the Cross* (Grand Rapids: Eerdmans, 2001), 159, 172.

Objective Foundation

Before examining the key passages, a word about the objective foundation of imitation is in order. The question, "What Would Jesus Do?" *must* be based on the answer to the question, "What Did Jesus Do?" In a similar though different domain of discourse, evangelical theologians often do wonderful work on the objective aspects of the atonement but neglect the subjective elements of the atonement. This is often because they are jealous to guard those objective elements (penal substitution, ransom, propitiation, etc.) against liberal theologians who deny these vital doctrines. Paige Patterson is typical in this regard; in a chapter on the work of Christ, he writes, "The Scriptures do say that the cross of Christ is an example of how to suffer righteously… nevertheless, a sustained argument establishing the central and most critical features of the atonement of Christ as being vicarious and substitutionary in nature."[7] Evangelicals often tip their hat towards this undeniably biblical theme, but rarely does one find a substantial treatment.[8] The emphasis

---

[7] Paige Patterson, "The Work of Christ," in *A Theology for the Church*, ed. Daniel L. Akin (Nashville: B&H Academic, 2007), 564. In a similar way in the same volume, Mark Dever writes, "Jesus' life does provide an example for Christian living. So say both Christ and the apostles (Mark 8:34; Matt. 10:25; 1 Pet. 2:21). But what sets Christian teaching apart from every other major religion is that its figurehead acts as both example and redeemer." "The Church," in *A Theology for the Church*, 782.

[8] Leon Morris, *The Cross in the New Testament* (Grand Rapids: Eerdmans,

of the New Testament doesn't fit the emphasis of most evangelicals in this regard. Notice the imbalance of Reformed theologian Michael Horton: "As heretical as it sounds today, it is probably worth telling Americans that you don't need Jesus to have better families, finances, health, or even morality."[9] Horton is right to call churches back to the importance of the doctrine of justification by faith alone, but as this booklet will demonstrate from the New Testament, you *do* need Jesus to have better families (Eph. 5:25ff), finances (2 Cor. 8:9), and certainly for better morality—otherwise the New Testament would not appeal to Jesus' example as often as it does.[10]

This booklet will not advocate moral*ism*, but it will advocate a Spirit-driven, cross-shaped, new covenant morality. Evangelicals are right to zealously guard the centrality of objective salvation. Without it, the imitation of Jesus would be futile, full-blown. As John Stott writes, "In the same way, the death of Jesus on the cross cannot be seen as a demonstration of love in itself, but only if he gave his life in order to rescue ours. His death must be seen to have had an objective before it can have an appeal....It was

---

1965), 322. Bruce Demarest gives one page to the moral example of Jesus in *The Cross and Salvation: The Doctrine of Salvation* (Wheaton, IL: Crossway, 1997), 182. Jason Hood's recent book *Imitating God in Christ* is a welcome start to remedying this problem.

[9] Michael Horton, *Christless Christianity* (Grand Rapids: Baker Books, 2008), 94.

[10] See Jason Hood, "Christ-Centered Interpretation Only? Moral Instruction from Scripture's Self-Interpretation as Caveat and Guide," *Scottish Bulletin of Evangelical Theology* 27, no. 1 (Spring 2009).

precisely in making a just satisfaction for sin that the manifestation of love took place."[11]

In the nomenclature of New Testament ethics, the imperative flows from the indicative.[12] As Richard Hays

---

[11] John R. W. Stott, *The Cross of Christ* (Downers Grove, IL: IVP Books, 2006), 216.

[12] Michael Parsons writes, "By 'indicative' we have in mind the fact that the new life in Christ is a work of God; it finds its origin in the death and resurrection of the Lord and comes into being through the work of the Holy Spirit. The believer is thus a new creation; a member of Christ; a temple of the Holy Spirit; he is regenerated, and so on. By 'imperative' we mean that the apostle also indicates that the new life thus given is to be continually manifested and worked out by the Christian believer." "Being Precedes Act: Indicative and Imperative in Paul's Writing," in *Understanding Paul's Ethics: Twentieth-Century Approaches*, ed. Brian S. Rosner (Grand Rapids: Eerdmans, 1995), 217. See the classic 1924 essay by Rudolf Bultmann, "The Problem of Ethics in Paul," in *Understanding Paul's Ethics: Twentieth-Century Approaches*, ed. Brian S. Rosner (Grand Rapids: Eerdmans, 1995); Frank J. Matera, *New Testament Ethics* (Louisville: Westminster John Knox Press, 1996), 136, 141. John M.G. Barclay, *Obeying the Truth: Paul's Ethics in Galatians* (Vancouver: Regent College Publishing, 1988), 226; Victor Paul Furnish, *Theology and Ethics in Paul* (Louisville: Westminster John Knox Press, 2009), 97, 224-27; T.J. Deidun, *New Covenant Morality* (Rome: Biblical Institute Press, 1981), 80-81, 228-29, 235; White, *Theological Foundations for New Covenant Ethics* (Frederick, MD: New Covenant Media, 2013), 41-46; idem, *The Law of Christ* (Frederick, MD: New Covenant Media, 2010), 11-47; Wolfgang Schrage, *The Ethics of the New Testament*, trans. David E. Green (Philadelphia: Fortress Press, 1988), 167-72, who writes, "God's eschatological act of salvation in Jesus Christ is the absolute basis, foundation, and prerequisite for all Christian conduct" (167); Brian Rosner, "Paul's Ethics," in *The Cambridge Companion to St. Paul*, ed.

writes, "Moral action is a logical entailment of God's redemptive action."[13] The *euangelion* grounds ethics.[14] One must hold these two truths together at all times. The indicative and the imperative are "closely and necessarily associated."[15] They cannot be separated without distorting the theology of the New Testament. A focus on the indicative without the imperative can produce licentiousness while the imperative without the indicative can produce legalism. Both are vitally necessary. This booklet will focus on the imperatival aspect of the cross, but the undergirding assumption is the indicative grounding. Evangelical exegetes and theologians must strive to be robustly cross-centered—seeing it as the objective source of

---

James D.G. Dunn (New York: Cambridge University Press, 2003), 217.

[13] Richard B. Hays, *The Moral Vision of the New Testament: A Contemporary Introduction to New Testament Ethics* (New York: HarperOne, 1996), 39.

[14] As Pastor Timothy Keller writes, "Religion operates on the principle of 'I obey – therefore I am accepted by God.' The basic operating principle of the gospel is 'I am accepted by God through the work of Jesus Christ – therefore I obey.'" *The Prodigal God* (New York: Dutton, 2008), 114. C.S. Lewis similarly writes, "There would be no sense in saying you trusted a person if you would not take his advice. Thus if you have really handed yourself over to Him, it must follow that you are trying to obey Him. But trying in a new way, a less worried way. Not doing these things in order to be saved, but because He has begun to save you already. Not hoping to get to Heaven as a reward for your actions, but inevitably wanting to act in a certain way because a first faint gleam of Heaven is already inside you." "Mere Christianity," in *The Complete C.S. Lewis: Signature Classics* (New York: HarperOne, 2002), 121.

[15] Furnish, *Theology and Ethics in Paul*, 223-24.

our salvation and the subjective shape of our Christian life, the power and paradigm for Christian existence.[16]

---

[16] This language comes from Michael J. Gorman, *Reading Paul* (Eugene, OR: Cascade, 2008), 78, 144.

Love

To speak of the imitation of Jesus is another way of speaking of biblical love. In contemporary culture, the term *love* is "notoriously ambiguous," meaning many things to many people.[17] It is most often defined as merely emotion; it comes and it goes. However, in the Bible, love is a verb.[18] First John 3:16 is perhaps the clearest biblical definition of love: "This is how we have come to know love: he laid down his life for us. We should also lay down our lives for our brothers."[19] Love can be defined as "a radical *giving* up of one's self and a radical *being given over* into the service of others,"[20] or put more simply, the giving of self for the good of others. However, such love in the New Testament is not without illustration. Michael Gorman notes, "Love has a

---

[17] Deidun, *New Covenant Morality*, 234; Gorman, *Cruciformity*, 157.

[18] Gorman, *Reading Paul*, 156.

[19] I have used the HCSB translation throughout this booklet, unless otherwise noted. One could also point to 1 John 4:10-11 as well: "Love consists in this: not that we loved God, but that He loved us and sent His Son to be the propitiation for our sins. Dear friends, if God loved us in this way, we also must love one another."

[20] Furnish, *Theology and Ethics in Paul*, 204; so also Gordon D. Fee, *God's Empowering Presence* (Peabody, MA: Hendrickson, 1994), 447; Matera, *New Testament Ethics*, 77; Gorman, *Reading Paul*, 157, 186; Schrage, *The Ethics of the New Testament*, 212. This definition, therefore, is wide enough to fit all of Paul's teaching on mutual upbuilding as well. See Furnish, *Theology and Ethics in Paul*, 234; Hays, *Moral Vision of the New Testament*, 144-45, 154; Gorman, *Cruciformity*, 160, 172, 232.

very specific meaning for Paul—conformity to the pattern of Christ's self-giving, sacrificial love on the cross."[21] "The crucified one has defined the meaning of love."[22] Gorman is also helpful in pointing out biblical love's two-dimensional character that we will see in text after text: "*Negatively*, it does not seek its own advantage or edification. It is characterized by status- and rights-renunciation. *Positively*, it seeks the good, the advantage, the edification of others. It is characterized by regard for them.... It is not self-centered but others-oriented."[23]

---

[21] Michael J. Gorman, *Apostle of the Crucified Lord: A Theological Introduction to Paul and His Letters* (Grand Rapids: Eerdmans, 2004), 123; idem, *Cruciformity*, 163, 215. Focusing on Paul, Furnish agrees: "Paul sees the meaning of love (both what God gives and asks) revealed first of all in the grand humiliation of Christ's incarnation and death." *Theology and Ethics in Paul*, 223; also Deidun, *New Covenant Morality*, 221-22; Richard B. Hays, "Christology and Ethics in Galatians: The Law of Christ," *The Catholic Biblical Quarterly* 49, no. 1 (January 1987): 274-75; Morris, *The Cross in the New Testament*, 171: Hays, *Moral Vision of the New Testament*, 202.

[22] James W. Thompson, *Moral Formation According to Paul* (Grand Rapids: Baker Academic, 2011), 164.

[23] Gorman, *Cruciformity*, 160, 170, 177, 214, 223. On this theme, it is hard to improve on Gorman's three chapters on "Cruciform Love" found in this book. He defines cruciformity as "conformity to the crucified Christ." *Cruciformity*, 4.

New Testament Texts

Before examining several key passages, a word about methodology is needed. The thesis of this booklet is not limited to the use of the word *imitate* (*mimētēs*). Such an approach would be myopic at best. It is the *concept* of imitation we are concerned with and, as will be shown, the concept is abundant.[24] Also, this booklet is not advocating imitating the earthly Jesus in everything he did, but the imitation of his self-giving love. Imitation in the New Testament is not exact copying but adopting a certain way of thinking, the Jesus mindset.[25] As Hood puts it, "Imitation is often a matter of sharing a mindset, direction or pattern rather than literal and precise duplication."[26] First, we turn to a couple of passages from the Gospels.[27]

---

[24] S.E. Fowl, "Imitation of Paul/of Christ," in *Dictionary of Paul and His Letters*, ed. Gerald F. Hawthorne, Ralph P. Martin, and Daniel G. Reid (Downers Grove, IL: InterVarsity Press, 1993), 428; Hood, *Imitating God in Christ*, 119; indeed, R.E.O White claims that "the imitation of Christ is, in truth, the nearest principle in Christianity to a moral absolute" and "remains the heart of the Christian ethic." *Biblical Ethics* (Atlanta: John Knox Press, 1979), 109.

[25] Hood, *Imitating God in Christ*, 11. As Thompson puts it, "Paul challenges his readers to imitate Christ not in concrete deeds but as a pattern of selflessness in all of their conduct." *Moral Formation*, 14. Or as Michael Gorman describes it, "non-identical repetition, by the power of the Spirit, of the narrative of Christ's self-giving faith and love that was quintessentially expressed in his incarnation and death on the cross." *Reading Paul*, 146-47; cf. Burridge, *Imitating Jesus*, 148.

[26] Hood, *Imitating God in Christ*, 132.

[27] The genre of the Gospels as ancient biographical texts (*bioi*) is outside the scope of this work, but could be adduced to support the thesis of the booklet. See Jonathan T. Pennington, *Reading the Gospels Wisely: A Narrative and Theological Introduction* (Grand Rapids: Baker Academic, 2012), 18-35, who notes, "ancient biographies, such as the Gospels, very consciously present their character *as one to be emulated*" (33). Cf. also Burridge, *Imitating Jesus*, 73-78; Hood, *Imitating God in Christ*, 69.

I Have Left You an Example—John 13

> *Before the Passover Festival, Jesus knew that His hour had come to depart from this world to the Father. Having loved His own who were in the world, He loved them to the end. Now by the time of supper, the Devil had already put it into the heart of Judas, Simon Iscariot's son, to betray Him. Jesus knew that the Father had given everything into His hands, that He had come from God, and that He was going back to God. So He got up from supper, laid aside His robe, took a towel, and tied it around Himself. Next, He poured water into a basin and began to wash His disciples' feet and to dry them with the towel tied around Him. He came to Simon Peter, who asked Him, "Lord, are You going to wash my feet?" Jesus answered him, "What I'm doing you don't understand now, but afterward you will know." "You will never wash my feet—ever!" Peter said. Jesus replied, "If I don't wash you, you have no part with Me." Simon Peter said to Him, "Lord, not only my feet, but also my hands and my head." "One who has bathed," Jesus told him, "doesn't need to wash anything except his feet, but he is completely clean. You are clean, but not all of you." For He knew who would betray Him. This is why He said, "You are not all clean." When Jesus had washed their feet and put on His robe, He reclined again and said to them, "Do you know what I have done for you? You call Me Teacher and Lord. This is well said, for I am. So if I, your Lord and Teacher, have washed your feet, you also ought to wash one another's feet. For I have given you an example that you also should do just as I have done for you." I assure you: A slave is not greater than his master, and a messenger is not greater than the one who sent him. If you know these things, you are blessed if you do them.* (John 13:1-17)

John 13 begins the so-called "Farewell Discourse" of Jesus to his disciples. As he prepares for the cross, *this* is the message he wants to leave his messianic community. And what a mind-derailing message it is. The Lord of the universe performs the activity of a slave. The Messiah behaves like a menial servant.[28] The Lord Jesus ties a towel around his waist, pours water into a basin, and begins to wash the dirty, malodorous feet of his disciples. The King of Israel stoops down to dry their feet with his towel. Unbelievable. Peter does what anyone would; he objects but Jesus knows what's best. They need to experience and see this enacted parable of servant-like love, which points forward to Jesus' ultimate act of cleansing through self-sacrifice (John 13:7-9).[29] As Paul will say—probably reflecting on this event—he assumed "the form of a slave" (Phil. 2:7). Jesus tells them they must wash one another's feet because their Teacher and Lord washed theirs. "For I have given you an example that you also should do just as I have done for you" (John 13:15).[30] Clearly, in a culture with pavement and shoes, the actual act of foot-washing is not required of Christians,[31] but self-sacrificial, servant-like love is.[32]

---

[28] D. A. Carson, *The Gospel According to John*, The Pillar New Testament Commentary, ed. D. A. Carson (Grand Rapids: Eerdmans, 1991), 462.

[29] Ibid., 463.

[30] Carson notes that the word used for "example" (*hupdeigma*) also suggests "pattern." *John*, 468. This will be important when we examine Galatians 6:2.

[31] Carson points out that "the heart of Jesus' command is a humility and helpfulness toward brothers and sisters in Christ that may be cruelly parodied by a mere 'rite' of foot washing that easily masks an unbroken spirit and a haughty heart." *John*, 468.

[32] Note Gal. 5:13 in this regard: "For you were called to be free, brothers;

Towards the end of this same chapter, Jesus gives his new commandment: "I give you a new command: Love one another. Just as I have loved you, you must also love one another. By this all people will know that you are My disciples, if you have love for one another." Anyone familiar with Torah would know that this commandment is not new.[33] It is found in Leviticus 19:18. What is new about the command is the "as I have loved you" aspect.[34] Jesus has just modeled the sort of love his people are to have towards one another and will soon show an infinitely more dramatic act of self-sacrifice on the cross. We are called to imitate our

---

only don't use this freedom as an opportunity for the flesh, but serve one another through love." A more literal translation would be: become slaves (*douleuete*) of one another through love. In a uniquely Christian paradox, freedom is found through slavery. As Luther put it, "A Christian is a perfectly free lord of all, subject to none. A Christian is a perfectly dutiful servant of all, subject to all." "The Freedom of a Christian," in *Martin Luther's Basic Theological Writings*, (Minneapolis: Fortress, 1989), 596. Michael Gorman uses the language of *"bonded* freedom" and *"liberating* service." *Reading Paul*, 155, 159. Also see Schrage, who writes, "Radical freedom does not consist in libertinism, but takes the form of service. Those who are free remain so only when they are also free of their freedom; their freedom evaporates when it is not also freedom for Christ and for others." *The Ethics of the New Testament,* 176; also see 173; cf. Furnish, *Theology and Ethics in Paul,* 204.

[33] Or as Matera puts it, "The newness of Jesus' commandment, however, derives from its christological and eschatological context.... The newness of the love commandment, then, derives from the example of the one who gives it and the time in which it is given." Matera, *New Testament Ethics*, 106-07.

[34] Meyer, *The End of the Law*, 286.

Lord in servant-like love. Following his example, we give of self for the good of one another.[35]

---

[35] This is also an important point for John in his letters. See 1 John 1:7, 2:6, 3:3, 3:7, 4:10-11, and 4:17. See my *Abide in Him: A Theological Interpretation of John's First Letter* (Frederick, MD: New Covenant Media, 2012) on these passages for further exposition.

Servants of All—Mark 10:42-45

Jesus called them over and said to them, "You know that those who are regarded as rulers of the Gentiles dominate them, and their men of high positions exercise power over them. But it must not be like that among you. On the contrary, whoever wants to become great among you must be your servant, and whoever wants to be first among you must be a slave to all. For even the Son of Man did not come to be served, but to serve, and to give His life—a ransom for many." (Mark 10:42-45)

Mark 10 is right in the middle of Mark's section on discipleship (Mark 8:27-10:52).[36] Recall the setting. The overly-zealous James and John approach Jesus with a request. They want to be at the top of the new world order, under Jesus, of course. Jesus rebukes them, saying in essence that they do not know what they are asking for. His kingdom "is not coming with something observable" (Luke 17:20); his kingdom "is not of this world" (John 18:36). His rule manifests itself in the opposite way his disciples expected.[37] He tells them that his way is not like the world. His way is *counter*-cultural. He says that pagans are known

---

[36] R.T France, *Divine Government* (Vancouver: Regent College Publishing, 1990), 49; Hood, *Imitating God in Christ,* 72-76; Hays, *Moral Vision of the New Testament,* 79-85.

[37] As Stott elegantly puts it, "They speak a different language, breathe a different spirit and express a different ambition. James and John want to sit on thrones in power and glory; Jesus knows that he must hang on a cross in weakness and shame. The antithesis is total." *The Cross of Christ,* 278.

for dominating those under them, and their leaders exercise power over their people.

"But," Jesus says, "it must not be like that among you. On the contrary, whoever wants to become great among you must be your servant, and whoever wants to be first among you must be a slave to all" (Mark 10:43-44). Jesus' messianic community is called to be a "not like that" kind of community. They are peculiar. They are a contrast society. As R.T. France puts it, "The natural expectations of society are reversed, and leadership is characterized by service, by being under the authority of others."[38] The disciples must recalibrate their internal definition of greatness. Christians are fundamentally called to be characterized by loving slavery to one another.

Jesus then grounds his moral instruction. For the purpose of this booklet, this is the important point of Jesus' teaching on self-giving service. His disciples are to be servants and slaves to all *because* (*gar*) "the Son of Man did not come to be served, but to serve, and to give His life—a ransom for many" (Mark 10:45). The reason given for why the disciples are called to loving service is because that is what Jesus did. He came to give of himself for the good of others. He came to be a ransom[39] for many.[40] R.T. France makes the obvious

---

[38] R.T France, *The Gospel of Mark*, The New International Greek Testament Commentary, ed. I. Howard Marshall and Donald A. Hagner (Grand Rapids: Eerdmans, 2002), 419.

[39] The language of "many" is alluding to the Suffering Servant (cf. Isa. 53:10-12). Space does not permit us to dip into the debate surrounding this word/concept. For a dated but double-bladed treatment, see Leon Morris, *The Apostolic Preaching of the Cross* (Grand Rapids: Eerdmans, 1965), 11-62. Also see R.T. France, "The Servant of

but important qualification that it is not the ransom for many "that they are expected to reproduce: that was Jesus' unique mission. But the spirit of service and self-sacrifice, the priority given to the needs" of the many, are for all disciples.[41]

---

the Lord in the Teaching of Jesus," *Tyndale Bulletin* 19 (1968), 26-52.

[40] A classic illustration of how the theme of imitation is often neglected is how often this passage is used merely as an "atonement" text rather than a "discipleship" text. As we will see with Philippians 2, there is doctrine explicated here, but the main point is how we should then live.

[41] France, *The Gospel of Mark*, 421.

The Jesus Mindset—Philippians 2:1-8

> *If then there is any encouragement in Christ, if any consolation of love, if any fellowship with the Spirit, if any affection and mercy, fulfill my joy by thinking the same way, having the same love, sharing the same feelings, focusing on one goal. Do nothing out of rivalry or conceit, but in humility consider others as more important than yourselves. Everyone should look out not only for his own interests, but also for the interests of others. Make your own attitude that of Christ Jesus, who, existing in the form of God, did not consider equality with God as something to be used for His own advantage. Instead He emptied Himself by assuming the form of a slave, taking on the likeness of men. And when He had come as a man in His external form, He humbled Himself by becoming obedient to the point of death—even to death on a cross.* (Philip. 2:1-8)

Philippians 2 is an extremely important passage. New Testament scholar Michael Gorman has made the case that this passage is Paul's "master story."[42] The literature this passage has produced is painstakingly voluminous.[43] For our purposes, it is quite straightforward.[44] Paul is calling the Philippian Christians to unity, and he appeals to the

---

[42] Gorman, *Apostle of the Crucified Lord*, 68, 102, 121, 315, 422, 431; idem., *Inhabiting the Cruciform God: Kenosis, Justification, and Theosis in Paul's Narrative Soteriology* (Grand Rapids: Eerdmans, 2009), 2, 12, 121; idem., *Cruciformity*, 168, 215.

[43] Gorman writes, "No passage in Paul, and perhaps no passage in the entire Bible, has received more scholarly attention than Philippians 2:6-11." *Apostle of the Crucified Lord,* 434.

[44] Those who deny an "ethical" reading of this chapter cannot do justice to the context of this hymn.

example of Jesus as he does so. In 2:2, he calls on them to have the same mindset (*to auto phrōnēte*),[45] to have the same love (*autēn agapēn*), being one-souled (*sūmpsūchoi*), and having one mindset (*hen phronountes*). Christians are to "consider others as more important than yourselves" (Philip. 2:3) and should look not only to their own interests but to the interests of others (Philip. 2:4). In other words, as we have seen, Paul is calling Christians to love.[46] After exhorting them to unity, Paul then commands them to have this mindset (*touto phrōneite*) among themselves which was also in Christ Jesus (Philip. 2:5), then explains what that mindset consists of: renouncing rights (Philip. 2:6: "did not consider equality with God as something to be used for His own advantage"), self-emptying (Philip. 2:7: "instead He emptied Himself"), and self-humbling (Philip. 2:8: "He humbled Himself"). This fits our definition of love perfectly: giving of self for the good of others. We can paraphrase the section this way: have the same mindset, that of looking not only to your interests but to the interests of others; have this mindset, like Jesus had, who did not look to his own interests but to the interests of others.[47] As Matera notes, "For Paul, Christians are to imitate the self-emptying of Christ."[48]

---

[45] Note that Paul uses almost the exact same phrase in Philippians 4:2 when he urges unity among Euodia and Syntyche: "I urge Euodia and I urge Syntyche to agree in the Lord" (better, have the same mindset – *to auto phrōnein*).

[46] Gorman, *Cruciformity*, 168; N.T Wright, *The Climax of the Covenant: Christ and the Law in Pauline Theology* (Minneapolis: Fortress, 1993), 87.

[47] Thompson, *Moral Formation According to Paul*, 106.

[48] Matera, *New Testament Ethics*, 179.

Gorman notes the structure of the passage and how the community of the Messiah is to imitate the Messiah, paraphrasing:[49]

    2:3-4 *Do not be selfish*

But in humility be selfless and consider others as more important than yourself.

    2:6-8 *Have the mindset of Jesus, who wasn't selfish*

But in humility emptied himself for the good of others (death on a cross).

Jesus had certain rights and prerogatives, but he didn't use them for his own advantage, but gave of himself for the good of others. This "pattern" is what should inform Christian behavior.

---

[49] Gorman, *Cruciformity*, 168, 256, 257.

The "Pattern" of the Messiah — Galatians 6:2

In Galatians 6:2 we read, "Carry one another's burdens; in this way you will fulfill the law of Christ." This is the only time the phrase "the law of Christ" occurs in Scripture.[50] This being the case, a precise definition is not readily clear, but the immediate context and the context of the letter as a whole makes it clear. First, it must be asserted that this phrase is *not* referring to the law of Moses.[51] In this letter, as well as in his other letters, Paul is explicitly clear that new covenant believers are no longer "under law"[52] (Rom. 6:14, 7:6, 10:4, 1 Cor. 9:20-21, Gal. 5:18, 2 Cor. 3).[53]

---

[50] Though, as we will see, a similar phrase is used in 1 Corinthians 9:21.

[51] Contra Matera, *New Testament Ethics*, 172.

[52] Contra Bruce W. Longenecker, *The Triumph of Abraham's God* (Nashville: Abingdon Press, 1998), 86, who regards the law of Christ as referring to the law of Moses since there are links between Galatians 6:2 and Galatians 5:13-14. This is also the approach of Graham Stanton, "The Law of Moses and the Law of Christ: Galatians 3:1-6:2" in *Paul and the Mosaic Law,* ed. James D.G. Dunn (Grand Rapids: Eerdmans, 1996), 99-116. John Barclay makes a similar error in *Obeying the Truth,* 132. He takes the law of Christ as the law redefined through Christ, *Obeying the Truth,* 134, 233. Todd A. Wilson does the same in his otherwise helpful overview of recent scholarship "The Law of Christ and the Law of Moses: Reflections on a Recent Trend in Interpretation," *Currents in Biblical Research* 5, no. 1 (October 2006): 134-37.

[53] For a clear treatment of Paul's view of the law, see Douglas J. Moo,

In Galatians he has declared that "the law is not based on faith" (Gal. 3:10). He shows that the law had a definite starting point (430 years after the promise to Abraham—3:17) and a definite ending point (until the seed/faith came—3:19). "The law, then, was our guardian until Christ" (Gal. 3:24). The word Paul uses here for "guardian" (*paidagōgos*) is best translated "babysitter."[54] In Greco-Roman households,

---

"'Law,' 'Works of the Law,' and Legalism in Paul," *Westminster Theological Journal* 45 (1983): 73-100; idem., "Paul and the Law in the Last Ten Years," *Scottish Journal of Theology* 40 (1987): 287-307; Jason C. Meyer, *The End of the Law: Mosaic Covenant in Pauline Theology* (Nashville: B&H Academic, 2009). Especially helpful is Meyer's treatment of the threefold problem of the law: anthropology, ontology, and chronology. See *The End of the Law*, 153; also see Thomas R. Schreiner, *The Law and Its Fulfillment: A Pauline Theology of Law* (Grand Rapids: Baker Books, 1993), 123-43; idem., *40 Questions About Christians and Biblical Law* (Grand Rapids: Kregel, 2010), 67-107; Stephen Westerholm, *Perspectives Old and New on Paul: The 'Lutheran' Paul and His Critics* (Grand Rapids: Eerdmans, 2004), 297-340; Longenecker, *The Triumph of Abraham's God*, 117-46; White, *What is New Covenant Theology?*, 19-38; idem., *Theological Foundations for New Covenant Ethics*, 29-32; idem., *The Law of Christ*, 51-74; John G. Reisinger, *Tablets of Stone and the History of Redemption* (Frederick, MD: New Covenant Media, 2004).

[54] Douglas Moo, "The Law of Christ as the Fulfillment of the Law of Moses: A Modified Lutheran View," in *Five Views on Law and Gospel*, ed. Stanley N. Gundry (Grand Rapids: Zondervan, 1999), 338; Thomas R. Schreiner, *Galatians*, Zondervan Exegetical Commentary on the New Testament, ed. Clinton E. Arnold (Grand Rapids: Zondervan, 2010), 238, 248, 255, 397; Meyer, *The End of the Law*, 173; Longenecker, *The Triumph of Abraham's God*, 126-28; N.T Wright, *Paul: In Fresh Perspective* (Minneapolis: Fortress Press, 2009), 97; John G. Reisinger, *Studies in Galatians* (Frederick, MD: New Covenant Media, 2010), 162; A. Blake White, *Galatians: A Theological Interpretation* (Frederick, MD: New Covenant Media, 2011), 81-85.

the guardian was distinct from the teacher. The guardian was the domestic slave responsible for supervising the child and taking the children to the teacher. Paul uses this metaphor to make a temporal point. The guardian is a temporary measure.[55] Once the children reach maturity, the babysitter has served its purpose.[56] For Paul, the law is part of the old age (Rom. 6:14); believers are no longer under the law but empowered by the gift of the new covenant, the Holy Spirit (Ezek. 36-37).[57] Clearly, therefore, the "law of Christ" is not the law of Moses.[58]

---

[55] Linda L. Belleville, "'Under Law': Structural Analysis and the Pauline Concept of Law in Galatians 3.21-4.11," *Journal for the Study of the New Testament* 26 (1986): 59-63; Richard N. Longenecker, "The Pedagogical Nature of the Law in Galatians 3:19-4:7, "*Journal of the Evangelical Theological Society* 25, no. 1 (March 1982): 53-61; Furnish, *Theology and Ethics in Paul,* 160.

[56] Space doesn't permit an exposition, but shockingly, Paul goes on to assert that to return to the law *after* the coming of Christ is tantamount to returning to demons! See Galatians 4:8-11.

[57] Longenecker, *Triumph of Abraham's God,* 83. Gorman writes, "Thus for Paul, depending especially on the prophets Jeremiah and Ezekiel, the old covenant was never intended to be permanent but to be renewed by a covenant involving God's Spirit." *Apostle of the Crucified Lord,* 299-300. Fee nicely sums up Pauline ethics: "God's glory is their *purpose,* the Spirit is their *power,* love is the *principle,* and Christ is the *pattern.*" *God's Empowering Presence,* 463; Deidun, *New Covenant Morality,* 219.

[58] The genitive "of Christ" rather than "of Moses" should make this point clear enough. See the incisive treatment by David G. Horrell, *Solidarity and Difference* (New York: T&T Clark International, 2005), 222-31; White, *The Law of Christ,* 128-31.

What, then, does Paul mean by "the law of Christ?"[59] In the immediate context, the law of Christ is related to bearing the burdens of others: "Carry one another's burdens; in this way you will fulfill the law of Christ" (Gal. 6:2). The "law" of Christ is the "law" of burden-bearing.[60] In other words, Paul is not referring to a literal "law" here.[61] He is using a word play on the word "law" to refer to a pattern[62] or

---

[59] Davies and his student Dodd are responsible for the view that the law of Christ is a new messianic Torah. See W.D. Davies, *Paul and Rabbinic Judaism* (Philadelphia: Fortress, 1980) and C.H. Dodd, "[*Ennomos Christou*]" in *More New Testament Studies* (Grand Rapids: Eerdmans, 1968), 134-48. For a critique of this popular view, see Deidun, *New Covenant Morality*, 171-75; Barclay, *Obeying the Truth*, 126-35; Hays, "Christology and Ethics in Galatians," 273-74, 286. Richard N. Longenecker defines the law of Christ as those "prescriptive principles stemming from the heart of the gospel (usually embodied in the example and teachings of Jesus) which are meant to be applied to specific situations by the direction and enablement of the Holy Spirit, being always motivated and conditioned by love." *Galatians*, Word Biblical Commentary, ed. Ralph P. Martin, vol. 41 (Dallas: Word, 1990), 275-76. Also see his "The Exercise of Liberty" in *Paul: Apostle of Liberty* (New York: Harper & Row, 1964), 181-208. Moo has a very similar definition: the law of Christ "does not consist of legal prescriptions and ordinances, but of the teaching and example of Jesus and the apostles, the central demand of love, and the guiding influence of the indwelling Holy Spirit." "The Law of Christ as the Fulfillment of the Law of Moses," 343.

[60] I am indebted to Hays, "Christology and Ethics in Galatians" for this whole section.

[61] James D. G. Dunn, "'The Law of Faith,' 'the Law of the Spirit' and 'the Law of Christ,'" in *Theology and Ethics in Paul and His Interpreters: Essays in Honor of Victor Paul Furnish*, ed. Eugene H. Lovering, Jr. and Jerry L. Sumney (Nashville: Abingdon Press, 1996), 64.

The "Pattern" of the Messiah—Galatians 6:2

mindset or principle demonstrated by Christ.[63] The law of Chris is his pattern of burden-bearing. As noted, this is another way of speaking of love: giving of self for the good of others, i.e., bearing their burden. From the beginning of the letter, the Messiah himself is the paradigmatic burden-bearer.[64] Jesus "gave Himself for our sins to rescue us from this present evil age" (Gal. 1:4). Jesus loved us and gave himself for us (Gal. 2:20). Jesus became a curse for us in order to redeem us (Gal. 3:13-14). In Galatians 4:4-7, God

---

[62] Matera, *New Testament Ethics,* 170; Richard B. Hays, *First Corinthians,* Interpretation (Louisville: Westminster John Knox Press, 2011), 154-55; Horrell, *Solidarity and Difference,* 229; Gorman, *Cruciformity,*173, 221, 266. Luke Timothy Johnson, who writes, "The *nomos Christou* (perhaps better translated not 'law of Christ' but 'pattern of the Messiah') is filled out by a mode of life that seeks the good of the other even at cost to oneself: bearing one another's burdens. The story of Jesus is the norm for the moral character of the community." *Living Jesus: Learning the Heart of the Gospel* (New York: HarperOne, 1999), 111.

[63] Hays, "Christology and Ethics," 275. Hays also suggests "regulative principle" and "structure of existence" and points to Romans 3:27 and Romans 8:2 where Paul also uses "law" as an "ironic rhetorical formulation." Also see Paul's use of law in Romans 7:25, 8:2, and Galatians 5:23.

[64] Fee writes, "Christ serves as the pattern for the principle, love itself. Thus, 'the law of Christ' is first of all an appeal not to some new set of laws or even to some ethical standards that the gospel imposes on believers, but to Christ himself, who in this letter has been deliberately described as the one 'who gave himself for our sins' (1:4) and who 'loved me and gave himself for me' (2:20)." *God's Empowering Presence,* 463; so also Longenecker, *The Triumph of Abraham's God,* 71; Hays, "Christology and Ethics," 277.

gives of self by sending his Son to redeem those under the law so that we might receive adoption.

So the law of Christ (or better, the pattern of the Messiah) is essentially the law of love,[65] and as we have seen, the cross of Christ gives explanation to love.[66] He loved us and gave himself for us (Gal. 2:20).[67] Therefore, in calling us to carry one another's burdens and fulfill the law of Christ, Paul is essentially calling us to imitate the self-giving love of Jesus that benefits others.[68] Though there are no explicit textual connections, more than likely Paul has Jesus' sacrificial foot-washing (which pointed forward to his sacrificial death) in mind when he speaks of the "law" of Christ. As Furnish puts it, "To imitate Christ means to give one's self in love for others as he gave himself. Love is therefore the 'law of Christ' (Gal. 6:2)."[69] The community of the Messiah is to follow "the narrative pattern of the crucified Messiah,"[70]

---

[65] Victor Paul Furnish, *The Love Command in the New Testament* (Nashville: Abingdon Press, 1972), 100; idem., *Theology and Ethics in Paul*, 64, 235; Tom Wright, *Paul for Everyone: Galatians and Thessalonians* (Louisville: Westminster John Knox Press, 2002), 76; White, *The Law of Christ*, 85-93.

[66] Thompson, *Moral Formation According to Paul*, 180; Hays, *Moral Vision of the New Testament*, 202.

[67] Gorman argues that the *kai* should be translated as "by" so the verse would read "who loved me by giving himself for me." *Cruciformity*, 219.

[68] Schrage, *The Ethics of the New Testament*, 208; Schreiner, *Galatians*, 335, 360, 400; Richard B. Hays, *Galatians*, The New Interpreter's Bible, vol. XI (Nashville: Abingdon, 2000), 333; Ben Witherington III, *Grace in Galatia* (Grand Rapids: Eerdmans, 1998), 423; Hays, *The Moral Vision of the New Testament*, 28.

[69] Furnish, *Theology and Ethics in Paul*, 235.

which, as with the Jesus mindset of Philippians 2:5-8, is the "pattern of renouncing one's own privileges and interests for the sake of others."[71]

---

[70] Gorman, *Apostle of the Crucified Lord*, 140, 220, 260. Elsewhere Gorman defines the law of Christ as "the narrative pattern of self-giving, others-regarding love of the crucified Messiah Jesus." Gorman, *Cruciformity*, 174, 176.

[71] Richard B. Hays, "Crucified with Christ: A synthesis of the Theology of 1 and 2 Thessalonians, Philemon, Philippians, and Galatians," in *Pauline Theology, Vol. 1: Thessalonians, Philippians, Galatians and Philemon*, ed. Jouette M. Bassler (Minneapolis: Fortress Press, 1994), 241; Gorman, *Cruciformity*, 175.

Because Even Jesus—Romans 15:1-7

> *Now we who are strong have an obligation to bear the weaknesses of those without strength, and not to please ourselves. Each one of us must please his neighbor for his good, to build him up. For even the Messiah did not please Himself. On the contrary, as it is written, the insults of those who insult You have fallen on Me. For whatever was written in the past was written for our instruction, so that we may have hope through endurance and through the encouragement from the Scriptures. Now may the God who gives endurance and encouragement allow you to live in harmony with one another, according to the command of Christ Jesus, so that you may glorify the God and Father of our Lord Jesus Christ with a united mind and voice. Therefore accept one another, just as the Messiah also accepted you, to the glory of God.* (Rom. 15:1-7)

Jason Hood writes, "In Romans 15:1-7, Paul draws on the pattern of the servant Messiah in order to guide the life of believers in a socially, racially, and theologically mixed community."[72] Romans 14-15 is Paul's exhortation for the mutual acceptance between the "strong" and the "weak" based on the example of Jesus.[73] The strong are probably those who realize that they are free to eat anything (14:2-3) and are no longer obliged to keep the Sabbath (14:5). The weak are those who feel the need to continue in these Jewish practices for the sake of conscience. Although he commands

---

[72] Hood, *Imitating God in Christ*, 121.

[73] Hays summarizes Paul's concern nicely: "Jesus was willing to die for these people, says Paul, and you aren't even willing to modify your diet?" *Moral Vision of the New Testament*, 28.

the strong to accept the weak, this does not prevent Paul from teaching the weak, since Paul sides with the strong theologically.[74] Regarding the Sabbath, he writes, "Each one must be fully convinced in his own mind" (Rom. 14:5).[75] Regarding food, Paul knows and is persuaded in the Lord that "nothing is unclean in itself" (Rom. 14:14, alluding to Mark 7:15).[76]

Romans 15:1-3 is most important for the thesis of this booklet: "Now we who are strong have an obligation to bear the weaknesses of those without strength, and not to please ourselves. Each one of us must please his neighbor for his good, to build him up. For even the Messiah did not please himself." In order to show the consistency and pervasiveness of Paul's call to imitate the self-giving love of Jesus, notice how Paul uses similar wording here as we have seen in other passages. Just a couple of chapters earlier, Paul spoke of "obligation": "Do not owe (*ōphēlete*) anyone anything, except to love one another, for the one who loves another has fulfilled the law" (Rom. 13:8). Here he says the strong have an obligation (*ōphēlomen*) to bear with the weak.

---

[74] Thomas R. Schreiner, *Romans*, Baker Exegetical Commentary on the New Testament, ed. Moises Silva (Grand Rapids: Baker, 1998), 746.

[75] This verse is a death knell for the system of Covenant Theology, which regards the Decalogue as God's eternal moral law. As shown above, Christians are not bound to the Ten Commandments. Also see Colossians 2:16-17; see Tom Wells, *The Christian and the Sabbath* (Frederick, MD: New Covenant Media, 2010), 63-80; Tom Wells and Fred Zaspel, *New Covenant Theology* (Frederick, MD: New Covenant Media, 2002), 211-57; White, *The Law of Christ*, 138-40.

[76] Furnish has shown the strong parallels in these chapters with the Sermon on the Mount in *Theology and Ethics in Paul*, 53. Without doubt, Paul had the teaching of Jesus in mind here as well.

Paul used the same word for "bear" (*bastazein*) here as he did in Galatians 6:2: "Bear (*bastazete*) one another's burdens, and so fulfill the law of Christ" (ESV).[77]

Echoing the call in Philippians 2 to "look out not only for his own interests, but also for the interests of others," here as well, mature Christians are not to please ourselves.[78] Love "is not selfish" (1 Cor. 13:5). Christians are called to please their neighbor, building them up. Thomas Schreiner notes that "neighbor" points back to 13:8-10 as well, "where love is the banner of Christian living."[79] Then in verse 3, Paul gives us a reason why we should not be selfish: because (*gar*) "the Messiah[80] did not please Himself."[81] Christians are called to

---

[77] Schreiner, *Romans*, 746.

[78] Douglas Moo notes, "We find the same pattern of teaching in Philip. 2:1-11, where Paul pleads for believers to follow Christ's example in preferring other's interests to their own in order to bring unity to the community." *The Epistle to the Romans*, The New International Commentary on the New Testament, ed. Gordon D. Fee (Grand Rapids: Eerdmans, 1996), 865.

[79] Schreiner, *Romans*, 746; also Thompson, *Moral Formation According to Paul*, 169; Moo notes that Paul's use of "neighbor"(*plēsion*) shows that Paul bases his command to the strong on the love command since "neighbor" is found in quotations or allusions to the love command in 13 of its 16 uses in the New Testament. *Romans*, 867.

[80] For some reason, most English translations (e.g., ESV, NIV, NET, NAS, NRSV) leave the definite article untranslated (*ho Christos*). The HCSB is better here.

[81] F.F Bruce, *Romans*, The Tyndale New Testament Commentaries, ed. Leon Morris (Grand Rapids: Eerdmans, 1985), 240; Moo, *Romans*, 866, 869; Furnish, *Theology and Ethics in Paul*, 220.

imitate their Lord, the "supreme example"[82] of giving of self for the good and upbuilding of others. James Dunn notes the coherence of Paul's teaching on the imitation of Jesus:

> To fulfill the law of Christ is to bear one another's burdens, which is a particular example of loving the neighbor, which fulfills the law. The point should be obvious: in the parallel train of thought, "the law of Christ" (Galatians) is equivalent to Jesus' refusal to please himself (Romans). Which presumably means that in Paul's mind "the law of Christ" includes some reference to Jesus' own example.[83]

Later in the chapter, Paul prays that God would allow them "to live in harmony" with one another, or more literally, have the "same attitude of mind" (NIV) or simply same mindset (15:5—*to auto phrōnein*). This is the same word Paul used in Philippians 2:2: "thinking the same way" (*to auto phronēte*), which is expounded in Philippians 2:5 as the mindset of Jesus (*touto proneite*) who gave of self for the good of others.[84] Clearly this is a pervasive theme of Paul's preaching and teaching.

---

[82] Schreiner, *Romans*, 747.

[83] James D. G. Dunn, "'The Law of Faith,' 'the Law of the Spirit,' and 'the Law of Christ,'" in *Theology and Ethics in Paul and His Interpreters: Essays in Honor of Victor Paul Furnish*, ed. Eugene H. Lovering, Jr. and Jerry L. Sumney (Nashville: Abingdon Press, 1996), 76. In quoting Dunn, the reader should know the author has significant disagreements with other areas of Dunn's theology.

[84] This idea of the church having the "same mindset" is obviously important for Paul. Also see Rom. 12:16 (*to auto ... pronountes*), Philip. 4:2 (*to auto phrōnein*), 2 Cor. 13:11 (*to auto proneite*). This is part of the realization of the new covenant. Jeremiah 32:39, in the context of the promise of the new covenant, reads, "I will give them one heart and one way so that for their good and for the good of their descendants after them, they will fear Me always."

This is all according to Christ Jesus (Rom. 15:5 *kata Christon Iēsoun*).[85] Earlier in this section, he speaks of walking "according to love" (14:15 *kata agapēn*).[86] Walking according to love is walking according to Christ Jesus. Paul began this section of exhortation with a call to "accept anyone who is weak in faith" and then wraps up this section commanding the strong and the weak to "accept one another, just as the Messiah also accepted you, to the glory of God" (15:7). The imitation of the self-giving love of Jesus is the ground for his call to love, unity, and acceptance in Romans 14-15. As Gorman puts it, "In Romans 15, Christ's dying is a paradigmatic act of burden-bearing and others-pleasing love that can engender a host of analogous acts by Paul and his communities."[87]

---

[85] For some reason, the HCSB adds the words "the command of" in Romans 15:5. Literally, it is "according to Christ Jesus," referring to his example. So the NET has "in accordance with Christ Jesus."

[86] Schrage, *The Ethics of the New Testament*, 211.

[87] Gorman, *Cruciformity*, 172.

Imitate Me — 1 Corinthians 9-11

> *Although I am a free man and not anyone's slave, I have made myself a slave to everyone, in order to win more people. To the Jews I became like a Jew, to win Jews; to those under the law, like one under the law — though I myself am not under the law — to win those under the law. To those who are without that law, like one without the law — not being without God's law but within Christ's law — to win those without the law. To the weak I became weak, in order to win the weak. I have become all things to all people, so that I may by every possible means save some. Now I do all this because of the gospel, so I may become a partner in its benefits.* (1 Cor. 9:19-23)

> *Give no offense to the Jews or the Greeks or the church of God, just as I also try to please all people in all things, not seeking my own profit, but the profit of many, so that they may be saved. Imitate me, as I also imitate Christ.* (1 Cor. 10:32-11:1)

Paul's letter to the Corinthians (chapters 8-11 in particular) is full of concern for the edification and building up of others, based on the pattern of the self-giving Christ.[88] We will only look at two passages: 1 Corinthians 9:19-23 and 1 Corinthians 10:32-11:1. In 1 Corinthians 9, the apostle's ministry, his "ways in Christ Jesus," are based upon the paradigm of the Messiah, who did not take advantage of his rights, but renounced them for the sake of others (Philip. 2:6-8).[89] As an apostle, Paul has the right to eat, drink, to have a wife, and to reap financial benefit, "however, we have not

---

[88] Ben Witherington, *Conflict and Community in Corinth* (Grand Rapids: Eerdmans, 1995), 212.

[89] Gorman, *Cruciformity*, 187.

made use of this right; instead we endure everything" (1 Cor. 9:12).[90] "The operative norm here is relinquishment of self-interest for the benefit of others."[91] Paul has shown that "although free, and always though an apostle, he has surrendered certain rights for the sake of the community."[92] Paul was free, but made himself a slave to all, so that he could win more people (1 Cor. 9:19).[93] Although free from the law,[94] he made himself like a one under the law. Although not without God's law, he became like those who

---

[90] Note the similarity in 2 Thessalonians 3:7-9: "For you yourselves know how you must imitate us: We were not irresponsible among you; we did not eat anyone's food free of charge; instead, we labored and struggled, working night and day, so that we would not be a burden to any of you. It is not that we don't have the right to support, but we did it to make ourselves an example to you so that you would imitate us." They had the "right" to support but gave up that right so as not to be a burden and as an example. He calls the Thessalonians to imitate their behavior. This is what it means to be "in-lawed to Christ" (1 Cor. 9:21) and to imitate Paul as he imitates Jesus (1 Cor. 11:1).

[91] Hays, *Moral Vision of the New Testament*, 42.

[92] Matera, *New Testament Ethics*, 150.

[93] Without justification, the ESV softens Paul's "slavery" (*edoulōsa*) language here with "made myself a servant to all."

[94] Furnish misses the point of 1 Corinthians 7:19 as referring to the law when Paul speaks of keeping the commandments of God. The verse reads, "Circumcision does not matter and uncircumcision does not matter, but keeping God's commands does." The first clue that Paul is not referring to the commands of the Mosaic law is that circumcision is one of those commands! Furnish, *Theology and Ethics*, 199. Later he goes on to say that the commands of the law only "have meaning and force insofar as they express the commandment to love." Furnish, *Theology and Ethics*, 202.

are without law. As mentioned above, Christians are not under the Mosaic law, but that does not entail Christians are without law altogether. Here Paul teaches that the law of God and the law of Moses are no longer equivalent in the new covenant. He says he is not under the law, but not "without God's law but within Christ's law" (1 Cor. 9:21), literally "in law to Christ" (*ennomos Christou*). Based on the preceding context, I take being in-lawed to Christ in the same way I take Galatians 6:2, namely being subject to the pattern of the Messiah.[95] Gorman writes, since "Paul imitated Christ in that he did not seek his own interest but, in love, sought the welfare of others, the 'law' of Christ to which Paul conformed must be the law or principle of 'not seeking one's own.' In other words, the law of Christ is the principle of rights-renouncing, others-oriented love. Being under the law of Christ for Paul means having his ministry shaped by Christ's paradigmatic status-denying, others-regarding love."[96] Paul became like the weak. He became all things to all people, so that he might save some. Paul is very flexible for the sake of others. He is a principled pragmatist. He can adapt and give up his own prerogatives, so that others might benefit by being saved. Although free, he makes himself a slave to all.[97]

---

[95] Gorman, *Cruciformity*, 185-86. See Witherington, *Grace in Galatia*, 424; Gordon D. Fee, *The First Epistle to the Corinthians*, The New International Commentary on the New Testament, ed. Gordon D. Fee (Grand Rapids: Eerdmans, 1987), 430.

[96] Gorman, *Cruciformity*, 186.

[97] Recall the similar teaching in Galatians 5:13: "For you were called to be

In the second passage, Paul confesses he is a people-pleaser. He says he tries "to please all people in all things" (1 Cor. 10:33).[98] This is the same thing he said just a few verses earlier in 10:24 ("No one should seek his own good, but the good of the other person") and in Romans 15:1 ("and not to please ourselves"). He said the same thing in Philippians 2 as well: we should consider others as better than ourselves. Again, this is clearly a regular part of Paul's moral instruction. Paul does not seek his own profit, but the profit of many so they may be saved (1 Cor. 10:33). In other words, Paul loved. He gave of himself for the good of others. Then, as we have seen again and again in Paul, he gives us the reason for his behavior. In 1 Corinthians 11:1 (another poor chapter break),[99] he writes, "Imitate me, as I also imitate Christ." Paul views himself as a mini-Jesus, a little Christ, a *Christ*ian, so to imitate him is to imitate Jesus.[100] The poor

---

free, brothers; only don't use this freedom as an opportunity for the flesh, but serve one another through love." Fee writes, "Jesus himself is the paradigm for such servanthood. Free, in order to become slave to all – this is surely the ultimate expression of truly Christian, because it is truly Christ-like, behavior." *The First Epistle to the Corinthians*, 426. See note 29.

[98] It is important to note that Paul is only concerned with pleasing people when it is for their upbuilding. When it comes to the truth of the gospel, he is rabidly opposed to people-pleasing (see Gal. 1:10, 5:12, Rom. 2:29, Philip. 3:3).

[99] Fee, *The First Epistle to the Corinthians*, 490; Fowl, "Imitation of Paul/of Christ," 429.

[100] Cf. 1 Corinthians 4:15-17. Note the similar teaching in 1 Thes. 1:6-7: "and you became imitators of us and of the Lord when, in spite of severe persecution, you welcomed the message with joy from the Holy Spirit. As a result, you became an example to all the believers in Macedonia and Achaia." Hays writes, "To imitate Christ is also to

chapter break tempts the interpreter to see this as a call to imitate Jesus in a generic way, but the immediate context is clear: we are called to imitate Paul and Jesus in their pattern of giving of self to please others. As Fee notes, "The emphasis here is certainly on the example of Christ, which for Paul finds its primary focus in his sacrifice on the cross."[101] We are called to imitate Jesus and Paul in that they do not seek their own profit, but the profit of many.[102]

---

follow the apostolic example of surrendering one's own prerogatives and interests." *Moral Vision of the New Testament*, 46.

[101] Fee, *The First Epistle to the Corinthians*, 490.

[102] The "profit of many" of 1 Corinthians 10:33 is parallel to "save" in 1 Corinthians 9:22.

Though He Was Rich— 2 Corinthians 8:9

Second Corinthians 8-9 is Paul's extended exhortation to give financially to the collection. In the middle of his exhortation, he grounds his appeal to give in the example of the rights-renouncing, self-giving love of Jesus: "For you know the grace of our Lord Jesus Christ: Though He was rich, for your sake He became poor, so that by His poverty you might become rich."[103] Notice the parallel to Philippians 2:6-8:[104] "Though he was rich" corresponds to "who [though] existing in the form of God."[105] "He became poor" is parallel to "He emptied Himself" and "He humbled Himself." "By His poverty you might become rich" is parallel to "becoming obedient to the point of death—even death on a cross" for our sins (our ultimate good). In our sacrificial giving, we are to imitate the generous gift (*charis*) of Jesus, who gave of self for the good of others.[106]

---

[103] Contra Victor Paul Furnish, who denies any appeal to the example of Jesus here. *II Corinthians*, The Anchor Bible, ed. William Foxwell Albright and David Noel Freedmans, vol. 32A (Garden City, NY: Doubleday and Co, 1984), 418.

[104] Here I am dependent on Gorman, *Cruciformity,* 170-71.

[105] I take *huparxōn* as a concessive participle. See Daniel B. Wallace, *Greek Grammar Beyond the Basics* (Grand Rapids: Zondervan, 1996), 634-35.

[106] Hood, *Imitating God in Christ*, 127.

As Christ Loved the Church— Ephesians 4:32-5:1 and 5:25-26

And be kind and compassionate to one another, forgiving one another, just as God also forgave you in Christ. Therefore, be imitators of God, as dearly loved children. (Eph. 4:32-5:1)

Husbands, love your wives, just as Christ loved the church and gave Himself for her to make her holy, cleansing her with the washing of water by the word. He did this to present the church to Himself in splendor, without spot or wrinkle or anything like that, but holy and blameless. (Eph. 5:25-27)

The Holy Spirit also appeals to the example of God the Father and Jesus the Son through Paul in his letter to the Ephesians. We are exhorted to be kind, compassionate, and forgiving, "just as God also forgave you in Christ" (Eph. 4:32). We image/imitate God as we imitate his character towards others. Chapter 5 is another unfortunate chapter break. There Paul continues his appeal: "Therefore, be imitators of God, as dearly loved children. And walk in love, as the Messiah also loved us and gave Himself for us" (Eph. 5:1-2a). Because we are dearly loved children, we are to imitate God.[107] As Luther put it, "It is not imitation that

---

[107] On the imitation of God, see Hood, *Imitating God in Christ,* 19-57; Burridge, *Imitating Jesus,* 145. For a Western defense of *theosis,* see Gorman, *Inhabiting the Cruciform God,* who defines *theosis* as "transformative participation in the kenotic, cruciform character of God through Spirit-enabled conformity to the incarnate, crucified, and resurrected/glorified Christ." *Inhabiting the Cruciform God,* 7. Cf. Graham Tomlin, *Spiritual Fitness* (New York: Continuum, 2006), 73,

makes sons; it is adoption that makes imitators."[108] Then the Apostle calls us to walk in love, not a mere feeling, not whatever we want it to be, but like the Messiah—who gave himself for our good.

Recall that Horton claimed "that you don't need Jesus to have better families."[109] Paul begs to differ. Here in Ephesians 5, we have marriage-transforming teaching because of the cross. In 5:25-26, Paul writes, "Husbands, love your wives, just as Christ loved the church and gave Himself for her to make her holy, cleansing her with the washing of water by the word." Husbands are called to imitate the crucified Christ in marriage. Notice again that Paul gives a clear and concrete definition of the type of love he is after: Jesus loved "and gave Himself for her" (Eph. 5:25). Jesus gave of himself for the good (sanctification and cleansing) of the church. The aim of a holy husband's life is to give of himself in order to make his wife holy. Without the cross as the powerful paradigm, Christian marriage would look quite different.

87, 108, 114. Keith E. Johnson has argued that Scripture directs us to imitate the Trinity (*imitation trinitatis*) in three ways, with the emphasis being on imitating the incarnate Son. "How Should We Imitate the Trinity?" speech delivered to Annual National Meeting of the Evangelical Theological Society, November 16, 2012, Milwaukee, WI.

[108] Quoted in Hood, *Imitating God in Christ*, 83.

[109] Horton, *Christless Christianity*, 94.

He Left Us an Example—1 Peter 2:21-23

> *For you were called to this, because Christ also suffered for you, leaving you an example, so that you should follow in His steps.* ²² *He did not commit sin, and no deceit was found in His mouth;* ²³ *when He was reviled, He did not revile in return; when He was suffering, He did not threaten but entrusted Himself to the One who judges justly.* (1 Pet. 2:21-23)

First Peter 2 is also an important passage for the theme of the imitation of Christ. There we are explicitly told that Christ left us an example "so that you should follow in His steps" (1 Pet. 2:21). Peter "presents Jesus as the ultimate example of a life lived in submission to God in a broken world resolutely opposed to God and his people."[110] Our Master suffered so we should expect the same.[111] "A disciple is not above his teacher" (Luke 6:40). Here we find a similar pattern: self-sacrifice for the good of others. When reviled, we—like Jesus—do not revile in return. We don't threaten but entrust ourselves to the One who judges justly.[112] In the next chapter, Peter writes that Christians should not pay back "evil for evil or insult for insult but, on the contrary,

---

[110] Hood, *Imitating God in Christ*, 148-49.

[111] Furnish, *Theology and Ethics in Paul*, 223. So also Hays: "To be Jesus' disciple is to obey his call to bear the cross, thus to be like him." *Moral Vision of the New Testament*, 197.

[112] For a superb treatment on the non-retaliatory nature of the Christian life, see Hays, *Moral Vision*, 317-346; also see Gorman, *Inhabiting the Cruciform God*, 129-160.

giving a blessing, since you were called to this"[113] (1 Pet. 3:9).[114] Jesus is our example.

---

[113] Note the parallel. He started the call to imitation with "for you were called to this" (2:21); then in his exhortation to live like Jesus in the next chapter, he also says "you were called for this" (3:9).

[114] Schrage, *The Ethics of the New Testament,* 272. I find it significant that Peter's teaching here has strong parallels with Paul's teaching in Romans 12, where he urges them to have the same mindset (12:16 *to auto phronountes*). There Paul commands believers to "bless those who persecute you; bless and do not curse" (Rom. 12:14). This theme was clearly important for the early church, which is not surprising since the Lord taught his followers to "bless those who curse you, pray for those who mistreat you" (Luke 6:28).

Conclusion

This booklet has argued that the New Testament calls believers to imitate the example of Jesus in his self-giving love. Though several more could be appealed to, we have examined nine clear passages of Scripture that explicitly exhort the church to this task. The community of the Messiah is to be characterized by rights-relinquishing, prerogative abandoning, self-interest sacrificing love based on the pattern of Jesus applied in a host of diverse situations. Not only is this theme biblically present, it is pervasive. The church ignores or neglects this robust theme to its own detriment. In conclusion, it is hard to improve on Luther, who had clearly immersed himself in this rich biblical theme:

> Although the Christian is thus free from all works, he ought in this liberty to empty himself, take upon himself the form of a servant, be made in the likeness of men, be found in human form, and to serve, help, and in every way deal with his neighbor as he sees that God through Christ has dealt and still deals with him. This he should do freely, having regard for nothing but divine approval.… "I will therefore give myself as a Christ to my neighbor, just as Christ offered himself to me; I will do nothing in this life except what I see is necessary, profitable, and salutary to my neighbor, since through faith I have an abundance of all good things in Christ."[115]

---

[115] Luther, "The Freedom of a Christian," 618-19.

Soli Deo Gloria

Scripture Index

Leviticus
19:18, p. 17

Isaiah
53:10–12, p. 20

Jeremiah
32:39, p. 38

Ezekiel
36–37, p. 29

Matthew
10:25, p. 5

Mark
7:15, p. 36
8:27–10:52, p. 19
8:34, p. 5
10, p. 19
10:42–45, pp. i, 19
10:43–44, p. 20
10:45, p. 20

Luke
6:28, p. 52
6:40, p. 51
17:20, p. 19

John
3:16, p. 11
13, pp. i, 15
13:1–17, p. 15
13:7–9, p. 16
13:15, p. 16
18:36, p. 19

Romans
2:29, p. 44
3:27, p. 31
6:14, p. 29
6:14, 7:6, 10:4, p. 27
7:25, 8:2, p. 31
8:2, p. 31
12, p. 52
12:14, p. 52
12:16, p. 38
13:8, p. 36
14:5, p. 36
14:14, p. 36
14–15, pp. 35, 39
15, p. 39
15:1, p. 44
15:1–3, p. 36
15:1–7, pp. i, 35
15:5, p. 39

1 Corinthians
4:15–17, p. 44
7:19, p. 42
9, p. 41
9:12, p. 42
9:19, p. 42
9:19–23, p. 41
9:20–21, p. 27
9:21, pp. 27, 42, 43
9:22, p. 45
9–11, pp. i, 41
10:32–11:1, p. 41
10:33, pp. 44, 45
11:1, pp. 42, 44
13:5, p. 37

2 Corinthians
3, p. 27
8:9, pp. i, 6, 47
13:11, p. 38

Galatians
1:4, p. 31
1:10, 5:12, p. 44
2:20, pp. 31, 32
3, pp. 29, 59
3:1–6:2, p. 27
3:10, p. 28
3:13–14, p. 31
3:19–4:7, pp. 29, 62
3:24, p. 28
4:4–7, p. 31
4:8–11, p. 29
5:13, pp. 16, 43
5:13–14, p. 27
5:18, p. 27
5:23, p. 31
6:2, pp. i, 16, 27, 30, 32, 37, 43

Ephesians
4:32, p. 49
4:32–5:1, pp. i, 49
5, p. 50
5:1–2, p. 49
5:25, p. 50
5:25 ff, p. 6
5:25–27, p. 49

Philippians
2, pp. 21, 23, 37, 44
2:1–8, pp. i, 23
2:1–11, p. 37
2:2, p. 38
2:3, p. 24
2:4, p. 24
2:5, pp. 24, 38
2:5–8, p. 33
2:6, p. 24
2:6–8, pp. 41, 47
2:6–11, p. 23
2:7, p. 24
2:8, p. 24
3:3, p. 44
4:2, pp. 24, 38

Colossians
2:16–17, p. 36

1 Thessalonians
1:6–7, p. 44

Scripture Index

2 Thessalonians
3:7–9, p. 42

1 Peter
2:21, pp. 5, 51
2:21–23, pp. i, 51
3:9, p. 52

1 John
1:7, 2:6, 3:3, 3:7, 4:10–11, p. 18
4:10–11, p. 11

Bibliography

Belleville, Linda L. "'Under Law': Structural Analysis and the Pauline Concept of Law in Galatians 3.21-4.11." *Journal for the Study of the New Testament* 26 (1986): 53-78.

Bruce, F.F. *Romans*. The Tyndale New Testament Commentaries, ed. Leon Morris. Grand Rapids: Eerdmans, 1985.

Bultmann, Rudolf. "The Problem of Ethics in Paul." In *Understanding Paul's Ethics: Twentieth-Century Approaches*, ed. Brian S. Rosner, 195-216. Grand Rapids: Eerdmans, 1995.

Carson, D. A. *The Gospel According to John*. The Pillar New Testament Commentary, ed. D. A. Carson. Grand Rapids: Eerdmans, 1991.

Deidun, T.J. *New Covenant Morality in Paul*. Rome: Biblical Institute Press, 1981.

Demarest, Bruce. *The Cross and Salvation: The Doctrine of Salvation*. Wheaton, IL: Crossway, 1997.

Dunn, James D. G. "'The Law of Faith,' 'the Law of the Spirit' and 'the Law of Christ.'" In *Theology and Ethics in Paul and His Interpreters: Essays in Honor of Victor Paul Furnish*, ed. Eugene H. Lovering, Jr. and Jerry L. Sumney, 62-82. Nashville: Abingdon Press, 1996.

Fee, Gordon D. *The First Epistle to the Corinthians*. The New International Commentary on the New Testament, ed. Gordon D. Fee. Grand Rapids: Eerdmans, 1987.

_____. *God's Empowering Presence*. Peabody, MA: Hendrickson, 1994.

Fowl, S.E. "Imitation of Paul/of Christ." In *Dictionary of Paul and His Letters*, ed. Gerald F. Hawthorne, Ralph P. Martin, and Daniel G. Reid, 428-31. Downers Grove, IL: InterVarsity Press, 1993.

France, R.T. *The Gospel of Mark*. The New International Greek Testament Commentary, ed. I. Howard Marshall and Donald A. Hagner. Grand Rapids: Eerdmans, 2002.

_____. *Divine Government*. Vancouver: Regent College Publishing, 1990.

Furnish, Victor Paul. *The Love Command in the New Testament*. Nashville: Abingdon Press, 1972.

_____. *II Corinthians*. The Anchor Bible, ed. William Foxwell Albright and David Noel Freedmans, vol. 32A. Garden City, NY: Doubleday and Co, 1984.

_____. *Theology and Ethics in Paul*. Louisville: Westminster John Knox Press, 2009.

Gorman, Michael J. *Apostle of the Crucified Lord: A Theological Introduction to Paul and His Letters*. Grand Rapids: Eerdmans, 2004.

_____. *Cruciformity: Paul's Narrative Spirituality of the*

Bibliography

Cross. Grand Rapids: Eerdmans, 2001.

_____. *Inhabiting the Cruciform God: Kenosis, Justification, and Theosis in Paul's Narrative Soteriology*. Grand Rapids: Eerdmans, 2009.

_____. *Reading Paul*. Eugene, OR: Cascade, 2008.

Hays, Richard B. *The Moral Vision of the New Testament*. New York: HarperOne, 1996.

_____. "Christology and Ethics in Galatians: The Law of Christ." *The Catholic Biblical Quarterly* 49, no. 1 (January 1987): 268-90.

_____. "Crucified with Christ: A synthesis of the Theology of 1 and 2 Thessalonians, Philemon, Philippians, and Galatians." In *Pauline Theology, Vol. 1: Thessalonians, Philippians, Galatians and Philemon*, ed. Jouette M. Bassler, 234-43. Minneapolis: Fortress Press, 1994.

_____. *First Corinthians*. Interpretation. Louisville: Westminster John Knox Press, 2011.

_____. *Galatians*. The New Interpreter's Bible, vol. XI. Nashville: Abingdon, 2000.

Hood, Jason B. "Christ-Centered Interpretation Only? Moral Instruction from Scripture's Self-Interpretation as Caveat and Guide." *Scottish Bulletin of Evangelical Theology* 27, no. 1 (Spring 2009): 50-69.

———. *Imitating God in Christ: Recapturing a Biblical Pattern.* Downers Grove, IL: IVP Academic, 2013.

———. "The Cross in the New Testament: Two Theses in Conversation with Recent Literature (2000-2007)." *Westminster Theological Journal* 71 (2009): 281-95.

Horrell, David G. *Solidarity and Difference.* New York: T&T Clark International, 2005.

Horton, Michael. *Christless Christianity.* Grand Rapids: Baker Books, 2008.

Johnson, Keith E. "How Should We Imitate the Trinity?" Speech delivered to Annual National Meeting of the Evangelical Theological Society, November 16, 2012. Milwaukee, WI.

Johnson, Luke Timothy. *Living Jesus: Learning the Heart of the Gospel.* New York: HarperOne, 1999.

Keller, Timothy. *The Prodigal God.* New York: Dutton, 2008.

Longenecker, Bruce W. *The Triumph of Abraham's God.* Nashville: Abingdon Press, 1998.

Longenecker, Richard N. *Galatians.* Word Biblical Commentary, ed. Ralph P. Martin, vol. 41. Dallas: Word, 1990.

———. "The Pedagogical Nature of the Law in Galatians 3:19-4:7." *Journal of the Evangelical Theological Society* 25, no. 1 (March 1982): 53-61.

Bibliography

Luther, Martin. "The Freedom of a Christian." In *Martin Luther's Basic Theological Writings*. Minneapolis: Fortress, 1989.

Matera, Frank J. *New Testament Ethics*. Louisville: Westminster John Knox Press, 1996.

Meyer, Jason C. *The End of the Law: Mosaic Covenant in Pauline Theology*. Nashville: B&H Academic, 2009.

Moo, Douglas J. *The Epistle to the Romans*. The New International Commentary on the New Testament. Grand Rapids: Eerdmans, 1996.

_____. *The Letters to the Colossians and to Philemon*. The Pillar New Testament Commentary. Grand Rapids: Eerdmans, 2008.

_____. "'Law,' 'Works of the Law,' and Legalism in Paul." *Westminster Theological Journal* 45 (1983): 73-100.

_____. "Paul and the Law in the Last Ten Years." *Scottish Journal of Theology* 40 (1987): 287-307.

_____. "The Law of Christ as the Fulfillment of the Law of Moses: A Modified Lutheran View." In *Five Views on Law and Gospel*, ed. Stanley N. Gundry, 319-76. Grand Rapids: Zondervan, 1999.

Morris, Leon. *The Apostolic Preaching of the Cross*. Grand Rapids: Eerdmans, 1965.

———. *The Cross in the New Testament*. Grand Rapids: Eerdmans, 1965.

Parsons, Michael. "Being Precedes Act: Indicative and Imperative in Paul's Writing." In *Understanding Paul's Ethics: Twentieth-Century Approaches*, ed. Brian S. Rosner, 217-247. Grand Rapids: Eerdmans, 1995.

Patterson, Paige. "The Work of Christ." In *A Theology for the Church*, ed. Daniel L. Akin, 545-602. Nashville: B&H Academic, 2007.

Pennington, Jonathan T. *Reading the Gospels Wisely: A Narrative and Theological Introduction*. Grand Rapids: Baker Academic, 2012.

Reisinger, John G. *Continuity and Discontinuity*. Frederick, MD: New Covenant Media, 2011.

———. *Studies in Galatians*. Frederick, MD: New Covenant Media, 2010.

———. *Tablets of Stone & the History of Redemption*. Frederick, MD: New Covenant Media, 2004.

Rosner, Brian. "Paul's Ethics." In *The Cambridge Companion to St. Paul*, ed. James D.G. Dunn, 212-223. New York: Cambridge University Press, 2003.

Schrage, Wolfgang. *The Ethics of the New Testament*. Translated by David E. Green. Philadelphia: Fortress Press, 1988.

Schreiner, Thomas R. *The Law and Its Fulfillment: A Pauline*

Bibliography

Theology of Law. Grand Rapids: Baker Books, 1993.

_____. *Galatians*. Zondervan Exegetical Commentary on the New Testament, vol. 9, ed. Clinton E. Arnold. Grand Rapids: Zondervan, 2010.

_____. *Romans*. Baker Exegetical Commentary on the New Testament, vol. 6, ed. Moises Silva. Grand Rapids: Baker Academic, 1998.

Stott, John R. W. *The Cross of Christ*. Downers Grove, IL: IVP Books, 2006.

Thompson, James W. *Moral Formation According to Paul*. Grand Rapids: Baker Academic, 2011.

Wallace, Daniel B. *Greek Grammar Beyond the Basics*. Grand Rapids: Zondervan, 1996.

Wells, Tom. *The Christian and the Sabbath*. Frederick, MD: New Covenant Media, 2010.

Wells, Tom and Fred Zaspel. *New Covenant Theology: Description, Definition, Defense*. Frederick, MD: New Covenant Media, 2002.

White, A. Blake. *Abide in Him: A Theological Interpretation of John's First Letter*. Frederick, MD: New Covenant Media, 2012.

_____. *Galatians: A Theological Interpretation*. Frederick, MD: New Covenant Media, 2011.

———. *The Law of Christ: A Theological Proposal.* Frederick, MD: New Covenant Media, 2010.

———. *Theological Foundations for New Covenant Ethics.* Frederick, MD: New Covenant Media, 2013.

———. *What is New Covenant Theology? An Introduction.* Frederick, MD: New Covenant Media, 2012.

White, R.E.O. *Biblical Ethics.* Atlanta: John Knox Press, 1979.

Wilson, Todd A. "The Law of Christ and the Law of Moses: Reflections on a Recent Trend in Interpretation." *Currents in Biblical Research* 5, no. 1 (October 2006): 123-40.

Witherington III, Ben. *Conflict and Community in Corinth.* Grand Rapids: Eerdmans, 1995.

———. *Grace in Galatia.* Grand Rapids: Eerdmans, 1998.

Wright, N.T. *The Climax of the Covenant: Christ and the Law in Pauline Theology.* Minneapolis: Fortress, 1993.

———. *Paul: In Fresh Perspective.* Minneapolis: Fortress Press, 2009.

Wright, Tom. *Paul for Everyone: Galatians and Thessalonians.* Louisville: Westminster John Knox Press, 2002.

www.ingramcontent.com/pod-product-compliance
Lightning Source LLC
Chambersburg PA
CBHW071953070426
42453CB00012BA/2242